## Introduction

In March 2011, U.S. Africa Command established Joint Task Force Odyssey Dawn (JTF OD) to lead the multinational response to the crisis in Libya. Under the leadership of Admiral Samuel Locklear and the provisions of two United Nations Security Council Resolutions, the scope of JTF OD rapidly expanded from its initial humanitarian aid related tasks to high intensity military operations to protect civilians.[1] While JTF OD was a limited contingency operation, the crisis in Libya represented a quintessential complex security environment of the twenty-first century. The complexity did not necessarily emanate exclusively from the Libyan regime, but from the operating environment as well. It included vague U.S. strategic guidance, a change in objectives and end states, an inexperienced combatant command with respect to orchestrating a coalition or planning kinetic operations, and a myriad of command and control challenges.[2] Despite the complexity of the operating environment of Operation ODYSSEY DAWN, the agility of the joint force to react to dynamic conditions and prove its mettle in terms of underwriting global security was undeniable.[3]

Central to the effectiveness of JTF OD was the joint force commander (JFC). The JFC demonstrated the ability to envision the conditions of the battle space that supported the strategic desired endstate. This enabled him to develop a comprehensive plan that facilitated a successful military operation despite the inherent fog and friction of such a complex operating environment. Although the range of military operations in the twenty-first century will vary in ends, ways, and means, what will be crucial for the joint force to achieve its objectives is the JFC. In order for the joint force to overcome the complex security challenges in the future operating environment, the joint force commander must possess operational vision, the essential quality for operational leadership.

To illuminate the significance of this leadership quality in comparison to the scores of other personal leadership traits that are important to the success of the JFC in the future security environment, a brief description of the complex security environment will be provided. Following this explanation, the concept of operational vision will be examined to gain an understanding of its value to the JFC and the success of a major operation or campaign in a complex security environment. To illustrate the importance of operational vision to the outcome of a military campaign or major operation, an examination of this leadership quality of two operational leaders will be presented. In conclusion, recommendations will be proffered that center on how to cultivate and enhance the leadership quality of vision within future joint force commanders so that the joint force is prepared to overcome complex security challenges within future operating environments.

## Background

Some argue that the twenty-first century operating environment is relatively no more complex than the environment in which the twentieth century world wars were waged. War has been and will continue to be a contest of human wills.[4] Furthermore, the political underpinnings of war will shape the future operating environment as they did previous wars. With that said, there is no shortage of assumptions about the changing character of war in the future operating environment. The National Security Strategy (NSS), the National Military Strategy (NMS), the Capstone Concept for Joint Operations (CCJO): Joint Force 2020, and the Joint Operating Environment (JOE) 2010 are only a few national and strategic documents that go to great length to describe the future operating environment and its associated complexity.[5] Within the context of this paper, the term future operating environment is used interchangeably with future security environment.

The future security environment in which the joint force will find itself embroiled will be viewed as complex due to a profusion of variables. These variables include adversaries that will operate through nefarious networks and employ multiple modes of warfare (e.g. conventional and irregular).[6] Additional complexity comes from the violent non-state actor, the emergence of which challenges the international diplomatic framework of the Westphalian nation-state and seeks to exploit the expanding globalization phenomenon.[7] The complexity of the operating environment is not exclusive to a U.S. adversary. The interconnectedness of the elements that comprise the operating environment creates an amorphous operating environment that transcends borders, cultures, populations, and religions.[8] Therefore, gaining a clear understanding of the interconnectedness of the various elements presents a significant challenge to the JFC – a challenge that involves considerable risk. The risk is the miscalculation of the relationship and the interdependence of the various elements. Adaptability of an adversary is another layer of complexity in the operating environment and further challenges the JFC. In addition to the environment, it is anticipated that an adversary will adapt to the strategy of the U.S. forces and its allies.[9] Consequently, the JFC will be expected to develop a solution that is adaptable to the operating environment and one that retains flexibility to be responsive to a transforming security challenge.[10] Proper operational vision is the means by which a flexible, supportable, and achievable solution is formed.

Another facet of complexity with which the JFC will have to contend is the "flattening" of the hierarchal construct of the levels of war. To conceptualize an operational idea in this environment, a JFC must possess a significant awareness of international politics and military acumen.[11] The formulation of a proper operational vision demonstrates both operational competence of the JFC and that the JFC has a clear understanding of the geopolitical environment as it relates to his assigned objectives. There is no universal or absolute set of leadership or personality traits that will guarantee success in the future. However, the enduring leadership quality that draws upon essential personality traits such as knowledge and experience, boldness, and strength of character is operational vision. The operational vision of the JFC is the fundamental leadership quality that links the strategic direction with tactical actions. This linkage will enable the joint force to overcome the complex nature of the future security environment.

## Discussion/Analysis

Having discussed the future operating environment and its associated complexity, it is now important to examine operational vision, its characteristics, and its significance to the JFC's attainment of the military operational objective. To start the discussion of this theoretical concept and its effect on operational leadership, it is appropriate to first briefly describe its relationship with how the joint force should be employed to achieve its operational objectives. Current joint operational warfare doctrine is nested in the theoretical construct of operational art— a methodology of which a JFC must have an understanding and ability to competently leverage to yield a favorable operational outcome.[12] In his monograph *Vulcan Anvil*, Professor James J. Schneider of U.S. Army School of Advance Military Studies postulated that operational vision is one of eight essential attributes of operational art.[13] While this paper is not intended to discuss the theory and practice of operational art, it is important to appreciate that the most indispensable element of operational art is the commander.[14] Although the role of the JFC is without equal in terms of the scope of his responsibility within the joint force, the most decisive quality that the commander provides to the joint force is his ability to formulate an operational vision that subsequently informs the other elements of operational art, such as operational design, operational idea, commander's intent, and ultimately the operational objectives.

4

The overall scope of this analysis is restricted to the operational vision of the JFC in terms of the planning, execution, sustainment, and termination of a specific major military operation or campaign. In this context, operational vision is specific to a combatant commander or a subordinate operational commander. While there are corollaries between strategic vision (e.g. that of the Chairman of Joint Chiefs of Staff (CJCS) or military service chief) and operational vision of a JFC, a comparative analysis of the distinction of these concepts is worthy of a separate thesis. Suffice to say, an effective operational vision is informed by the strategic vision and the desired end state set by the political leadership.

As part of examining operational vision and its characteristics, it is necessary to begin with discussion of the most prevalent source of confusion about this concept within the joint force. The source of confusion and most influential challenge of understanding operational vision is the lack of a coherent or common doctrinal foundation for this concept within the joint force. The two most relevant publications on planning, conducting, sustaining, and terminating joint military operations are Joint Publication (JP) 3-0, *Operations* and JP 5-0, *Joint Operation Planning*. In JP 3-0, vision is discussed with respect to operational design and operation art[15] and is mentioned as important to the operational function of command and control.[16] In JP 5-0, the commander's vision is discussed in relation to the joint operational planning process.[17] Additionally, through the application of operational art, the commander's vision is noted as providing the theoretical framework to link tactics and policy.[18] Despite the incontrovertible importance of operational vision to planning, conducting, sustaining, and terminating military operations or campaigns, neither of the noted joint publications provides a clear and concise definition of what is meant by the concept.

Since the JFC comes from a U.S. military service and the JFC is expected to formulate a vision for the joint force with respect to its objective, the next most logical place to search for a definition of operational vision is a service doctrinal publication. The following publications were reviewed for either a definition or explanation of the concept of vision, specifically as it relates to operational leadership: MCDP-1 *Warfighting*, NDP-1 *Naval Warfare*, AFDD 3-1 *Air Warfare*, and ADP 3-0, *Unified Land Operations*. Additional rationale for examining the aforementioned publications was that each doctrinal publication described the services' respective warfighting philosophies, which all include the component of leadership. The common theme throughout each publication is the relationship of vision to various phases of operational planning and the concept is oriented toward a future desired end state. With that said, the reader is left to construct his interpretation of this concept and apply a subjective value to this unique concept within the art of operational leadership.

The U.S. Army Field Manual on Army Leadership (FM 6-22) provides a general explanation of the concept of vision as "another way that leaders can provide purpose."[19] The FM 6-22 also differentiates the levels of leadership as direct, organizational, and strategic.[20] In terms of vision, FM 6-22 states, "while direct and organizational level leaders provide purpose or intent, strategic leaders usually provide long-term vision or conceptual models."[21] From this, it is appropriate to infer that the application of the concept of vision is essentially only germane to a strategic leader. Although vision as it relates to a strategic leader is covered in great detail in this manual, the manual offers no demarcation between "vision" of a strategic leader (e.g. Army Chief of Staff) and an operational leader (e.g. joint force commander). Even though there are similarities between strategic and operational vision, a distinction exists in terms of scope, magnitude, and endstate. For instance, strategic vision is generally pertinent to change over a long period, whereas operational vision is specific to a major operation or military campaign. Although FM 6-22 provides a broad overview of vision within a general context, it does not address the concept of operational vision as it relates to operational leadership. Now that the doctrinal challenge of understanding operational vision has been discussed, it is appropriate to examine a posited theoretical explanation of operational vision and discuss its relevancy to effective operational leadership in the twenty-first century.

So what is operational vision? Dr. Milan Vego, a professor at the U.S. Naval War College and noted naval theorist, has provided a relevant theoretical description of operational vision and its characteristics. Vego has stated that operational vision is the "combination of the operational commander's personality traits, professional education and training, and experience."[22] By and large, these attributes form the framework of this concept. Utilizing these attributes, the JFC must envision the conditions within the operating environment "that will exist after the assigned mission is accomplished and of how to properly orchestrate the employment of forces"[23] to achieve the operational objective in support of the desired strategic endstate. The tangible result of this cognitive demand on the JFC is suffused through every element of the operational design process. In an attempt to add perspicuity to this seemingly abstract concept, Vego offered key elements of operational vision: "broad outlook, imagination, inner perspective, historical perspective, and determination."[24] Vego's description of operational vision is more than sufficient to address the void of a comprehensive explanation of this concept in joint doctrine. His description provides a theoretical foundation for the services to consider in terms of leadership development of joint force commanders.

A precise definition of operational vision is difficult to encapsulate given the myriad of factors that comprise this concept. Nevertheless, the following are characteristics that are germane to operational vision: (1) oriented toward desired endstate, (2) fundamental to effective operational leadership, (3) provides direction for the joint force, and (4) essential to joint planning.[25] It is imperative to note while operational vision is necessary to establish military operational objectives, the essence of operational vision is that the objectives must directly support attainment of the strategic desired end state. Utilizing Vego's description and the aforementioned characteristics, proper operational vision should demonstrate a JFC's holistic view of the operating environment, how he plans to employ military forces and coordinate non-military instruments of power, and how he the military objectives support the desired strategic endstate. Now that operational vision has been sufficiently explained, its relevance to operational leadership in the twenty-first century operating environment will be briefly discussed.

As pointed out earlier, operational vision is vital to the theoretical and doctrinal foundation of operational art. This is important to appreciate because operational vision is critical to an enduring principle of joint planning – the commander's intent. The concept of commander's intent is about leveraging the initiative of the subordinate commander and facilitating his freedom of action. The importance of the commander's intent is unquestionable, especially in the future security environment. Informed by the JFC's operational vision, the commander's intent is one of three key pillars of the Chairman of the Joint Chiefs of Staff's command philosophy for the future force aptly referred to as "mission command" (the other two pillars are understanding and trust).[26] The author suggests that operational vision is the critical link that binds all three pillars within the province of operational leadership. An intrinsic quality of proper operational vision of a JFC is the "understanding" of the operating environment and the desired end state. The operating environment includes the geopolitical landscape, as well as the physical and virtual domains in which the joint force will operate. As previously discussed operational vision informs the commander's intent, which is clearly influenced by the pillar of "understanding." Lastly, the communication of the operational vision to the joint force staff and subordinate commanders rides the proverbial bridge of "trust." This bridge travels in both directions in terms of the JFC and the joint force, as well as horizontally throughout the joint force and/or coalition. The quality of "trust" enables the JFC's operational vision to be a shared vision, which inevitably proves to be a potently orienting capability in relation to the objective for the joint force and subordinate commanders in a complex security environment.

Operational vision is a vital leadership quality for a JFC in the future security environment that will demand an adaptive joint force. Success of the joint force will require a JFC with the operational vision to leverage capabilities, resources, and networks to develop innovative solutions to complex problems. Having discussed operational vision and its relevance to effective operational leadership in the future security environment, an examination of two operational leaders and the effects of their vision to the outcome of their respective campaigns will be presented to illustrate the importance of this theoretical concept to operational leadership in a complex environment.

The following analysis of the operational vision of two operational commanders is not meant to evaluate the indispensable nature of this quality to operational leadership. In principle and doctrine, "vision" is a critical component to leadership no matter the scope of mission or size of an organization. The aim of this operational leadership analysis is to examine the efficacy of operational vision in a complex operating environment by utilizing three criteria: (1) did the JFC's operational vision demonstrate a holistic view of the operating environment, (2) did the JFC's operational vision provide a framework for the development and execution of a coherent plan, and (3) did the military objectives support the desired strategic end state? These questions were selected due to their applicability to success of the joint force in a future security environment. First, the operational vision of Lieutenant General Jagjit Singh Aurora will be analyzed. He was the operational commander for the Indian Army Eastern Command in the Indo-Pakistan War of 1971.[27] This will be followed by analysis of the operational vision of General Tommy Franks during the U.S. led war in Afghanistan from 2001-2003. The analysis

9

will demonstrate the complexity of each operating environment and will examine the commanders' operational vision as it related to the planning and execution of their respective campaigns utilizing the previous listed criteria. The analysis will conclude by considering the linkage between operational vision and the outcome of the campaign within a complex security environment.

In order to add context to third Indo-Pakistan War, it is important to understand the strategic setting. In March 1971, the Pakistani government decisively defeated a rebellion in East Pakistan. In the aftermath of Pakistani success, millions of refugees crossed the border into India.[28] As a result of the ensuing refugee crisis in India and the overwhelming burden to the India government, Indian military forces invaded East Pakistan in December 1971 in support of an autonomous nation of East Pakistan. The Indian defeat of Pakistani forces "liberated" East Pakistan, which eventually resulted in the independence of East Pakistan (now known as Bangladesh).[29]

In terms of complexity within the operating environment, India and Pakistan were supported by the world's two superpowers: Soviet Union and the United States. Additionally, India had to consider the potential of Chinese military forces coming to the aid of Pakistan after Chinese Premier Chou En-Lai declared his to support the government of Pakistan following its defeat of the rebellion.[30] An additional layer of complexity was the number, and types of forces LtGen Aurora commanded in East Pakistan. He commanded nearly 500,000 conventional and irregular forces comprised of former East Pakistani Rebel Forces and thousands of East Pakistani refugees who were armed and trained to serve as guerrilla forces.[31] While it would be wrong to assume that the future security environment will assuredly contain similar complexities, it would be unwise not to garner the lessons learned in terms of the value of operational vision to overcoming difficulties in a complex operating environment.

Lieutenant General Aurora was the operational commander responsible for developing and executing Operation WINDFALL, the Indian plan to invade East Pakistan and defeat Pakistani military forces in East Pakistan, whereby setting the conditions for a political solution to the secessionist movement in that country. Lieutenant General Aurora's operational vision directly contributed to the operational and strategic successes of Operation WINDFALL. To support this supposition, the first criterion to examine is whether his operational vision demonstrated a holistic view of the operating environment. His understanding of the geopolitical landscape and the operating environment can be inferred from the operational plan that facilitated a quick decisive victory. Lieutenant General Aurora knew that any escalation of hostilities between the Pakistan and India would garner international attention and influence from the United Nations, the Soviet Union, and the United States. As a result, LtGen Aurora needed a military strategy that delivered the political objective prior to international intervention.[32] Also, LtGen Aurora leveraged the advantages of using East Pakistan irregular and guerrilla forces due to their cultural and terrain expertise.[33] Furthermore, the utilization of East Pakistani citizens to fight for their own independence would underscore the legitimacy of self-determination in south Asia post-European colonial rule.[34] These aspects of his operational plan demonstrate his holistic view of the operating environment.

The second criterion to discuss is whether his operational vision provided the framework for the development and execution of a coherent plan, which included the Indian military's first application of maneuver warfare.[35] Lieutenant General Aurora drew upon his experience, knowledge, and boldness to paint a picture of the future end state that engendered a sense of shared vision among his subordinate commanders to "buy in" to this new warfare concept. Despite the complexity of his operational design that included the sequencing and maneuvering of four corps sized units spread over 1500 miles along exterior lines of operation to the outskirts of the city of Dacca (capital of East Pakistan and location of Pakistani Forces headquarters) and an airborne drop of a paratrooper battalion at the climax of hostilities, LtGen Aurora's operational vision was the instrument that focused the subordinate commanders on the objectives in a challenging operating environment.[36]

The last criterion to examine is whether the military objectives supported the desired strategic endstate, which were an autonomous East Pakistan and the emergence of India as a hegemonic contender in south Asia.[37] Focused on the desired endstate, LtGen Aurora formulated an appropriate operational vision and subsequent commander's intent that allowed freedom of action for his subordinate commander's to seize the initiative upon presentation of favorable opportunities. An example was the improvisation of a "complicated air mobile landing" along the northern axis of advance to Dacca.[38] Another illustration of the nexus of the military objectives and the desired endstate was the rapid decisive defeat of Pakistani military forces in East Pakistan. A protracted contest would not have achieved the desired endstate. Therefore, LtGen Aurora's operational vision led to an operational design in which the objectives achieved clearly supported the desired endstate.

In the 1971 Indo-Pakistan War, LtGen Aurora's operational vision was that essential leadership quality that enabled his joint force to overcome the challenges of a complex operating environment. His operational vision demonstrated a holistic view of the operating environment and provided a framework for an effective operational plan to achieve military objectives that were in consonance with the desired endstate. After analyzing the 1971 Indo-Pakistan War case study and demonstrating the linkage of proper operational vision to the outcome of a campaign within a complex operating environment, it is appropriate to examine a contemporary case study that has its own set of complexities that continue to influence the "developing outcome" for the United States.

The international political setting prior to U.S. military operations in Afghanistan largely favored a response to the September 11, 2001 terrorist attacks against the United States. This recognition adds context to the 2001 U.S.-led invasion into Afghanistan. In less than a month after the terrorist attacks in New York and Washington, D.C., U.S. Central Command (USCENTCOM) developed and executed a military strategy that (1) destroyed al-Qaeda (AQ) in Afghanistan, and (2) removed the Taliban regime.[39] Within two months, the military objectives were achieved, and Afghanistan was under an interim government authority backed by the United Nations (UN).[40] Despite the initial tactical success, the United States remains engaged in combat operations in Afghanistan twelve years after affecting a regime change.

Even though the U.S. military objectives were accomplished in a relatively rapid manner, it is important to acknowledge the complexities of the operating environment. In *American Soldier*, General Franks stated that on September 12, 2001, USCENTCOM had no plan "for conventional ground operations in Afghanistan."[41] The crisis action planning that ensued was further complicated by U.S. political demands for time-sensitive military options because the United States needed to preserve its preeminence as a world superpower and the potential threat of further terrorist attacks was not foreclosed. The physical characteristics of Afghanistan presented another layer of complexity to U.S. war planners, especially in terms of the lack of force staging options within the region to support a ground invasion.[42] In addition to major combat operations, war planners had to consider the potential humanitarian disaster after the departure of non-governmental organizations (NGOs) from the joint operating environment (JOA).[43] Lastly, the JFC had to contend with two separate adversaries, each of whom had its own strategic aims. As with the previous case study, the description of the challenges, while not exhaustive, is illustrative of a complex future security environment. The value of a JFC's operational vision to the strategic outcome of a military campaign in the future security environment can be determined by examining the first U.S. military campaign of the twenty-first century.[44]

For the U.S. led invasion to Afghanistan in 2001, Operation ENDURING FREEDOM (OEF), General Franks was both the geographic combatant commander and joint force commander. General Franks' concept of operations (CONOPS) included four phases and relied extensively on indigenous anti-Taliban tribal forces (Northern Alliance), supported by special operations forces (SOF) and other intelligence operatives, and U.S. air power.[45] Utilizing the same evaluation criteria as in the previous case study, General Franks' operational vision will be examined by first addressing whether his vision demonstrated a holistic view of the operating environment. Given the constraints of time, limited allocation of forces, the geo-political challenges to leveraging U.S. regional partners for support, and the need to "liberate" rather than "occupy" a sovereign nation, General Frank's operational vision only partially demonstrated a holistic view of the operating environment. General Franks envisioned a small footprint of specialized and conventional forces that would "seek out and eliminate pockets of resistance."[46] His vision proved ineffective as the Taliban was neither defeated nor eliminated, and AQ forces were displaced across the border into Pakistan.[47] The re-emergence of these U.S. adversaries in Afghanistan would result in much larger footprint of U.S. military forces to Afghanistan starting in 2008. While it can be argued that their re-emergence occurred while the Afghanistan war effort was under the management of the United Nations, General Franks' limited operational vision prevented tactical gains from being exploited for strategic success.

The second criterion examined is whether General Franks' operational vision provided a framework for the development and execution of a coherent plan. The short answer is "no" based on the plan's objective to defeat AQ and the Taliban. In spite of the phased approach to executing the initial Afghanistan campaign, the plan was limited to reflect a counterterrorism

14

strategy versus a viable war strategy that reflected prioritization and resourcing of Phase IV and Phase V operations.[48] While General Franks' operational vision was clearly informed by the Soviet experience in Afghanistan in terms of the number of conventional forces that fought against the mujahedeen,[49] his plan lacked coherency with respect to what was to be done after the military objectives were achieved. The responsibility of the joint force commander is to develop a war strategy that links tactical actions to policy objectives. General Franks' strategy was narrowly limited, did not lead to the defeat of the adversaries, and did not sufficiently enable civil authority.

The last criterion to be discussed with respect to General Franks' operational vision is whether the military objectives supported the desired strategic endstate. In terms of developing an operational vision, a clear, achievable strategic desired end state is essential. For the initial invasion into Afghanistan, some argue that General Franks was given vague political guidance concerning Afghanistan post-Taliban rule, which resulted in a flawed military strategy.[50] While the debate continues on that issue, it can be inferred that General Franks had a clear understanding of what he perceived to be that endstate. His operational vision translated the policy goals into military objectives, which included the efforts in support of stability operations (e.g., nation building). Regardless of the strategic guidance given to him, General Franks was responsible for setting the conditions that would result in a favorable outcome for the U.S. after the military objectives were achieved. His inability to properly visualize the conditions that succeeded the transition from Phase III to Phase IV operations and his decision to assign a less than sufficient size force to effectively conduct Phase IV operations have resulted in the U.S.' involvement in its longest sustained conflict.

Like the previous case study, the JFC's operational vision has had a significant impact on the military campaign. General Franks' operational vision relied on an unconventional approach that did not demonstrate a holistic view of the operating environment, which included an adaptive adversary. His envisioned plan did not sufficiently address the evolving security challenge or adequately allocate the appropriate force capability to support all phases of joint operations. The lack of an overall national strategy for a post-Taliban Afghanistan notwithstanding, General Franks' operational vision resulted in a military strategy that garnered an unfavorable outcome for the United States in terms of a better state of peace.

## CONCLUSION/RECOMMENDATIONS

The analysis demonstrates that the JFC's operational vision is the essential leadership quality that will enable a joint force to overcome a security environment that has been described by the Chairman of the Joint Chiefs of Staff as "dangerous, unpredictable, and increasingly competitive."[51] This environment will require a responsive, adaptive joint force that is capable of successfully executing missions across range of military operations. The key to the success of this joint force is the JFC who possesses the operational vision that transcends traditional approaches to problem solving. The operational vision needed will be the manifestation of the JFC's understanding of the operating environment and the development of a coherent, flexible plan that is firmly nested with policy objectives.

The formulation of proper operational vision in a future security environment will not be a simple task. In his reflection on his initial strategy as the operational commander for the war in Iraq in 2004, General George E. Casey, Jr. noted that in an uncertain and complex security environment, the most difficult task for leaders is to attain mental clarity on the objectives for their subordinates.[52] The foundation for operational vision is professional experience, education, training, and individual personality traits (e.g. boldness, character, integrity). Given this foundation, the following are two recommendations to ensure future JFCs have the operational vision necessary to better lead the joint force.

16

First, joint doctrine should provide a clear theoretical foundation of the concept of operational vision and its relationship to the roles and responsibilities of the JFC. The inclusion of a description of this theoretical concept within a joint publication will facilitate a common understanding across the joint force and by future joint force commanders. Lastly, its inclusion within joint doctrine ensures that its value to and relation with operational art is firmly understood by the joint force.

Secondly, and in spite of the current measures to for the Department of Defense (DOD) to become more fiscally prudent, resources dedicated to the development of future joint force commanders must be preserved to the greatest extent possible. In order for the U.S. military to proclaim its forces are best led, it needs to ensure that it continues education and training initiatives that enable its future joint force commanders to fulfill the many facets of leadership. An example is to increase U.S. military officers' exposure to the other instruments of national power, specifically in relation to efforts in support of the national security strategy. In this example, the purpose is two-fold: DOD recognizes the roles and responsibilities of the other instruments and it strengthens relationships between the U.S. military and other governmental agencies (OGAs). With respect to professional education, opportunities for senior officers to attend top-tier civilian graduate schools should be explored. The purpose would be to develop and improve critical thinking skills and expose future JFCs to disciplines that are relevant to the future operating environment, such as "anthropology, economics, geopolitics, cultural studies, the 'hard' sciences, law, and strategic communication."[53]

The future security environment obliges the JFC to understand and demonstrate operational vision. Operational vision embodies purpose and while having proper operational vision does not guarantee success for the JFC, lacking it all but assures failure.

Gregory James, Larry Holcomb, and Chad Manske, "Joint Task Force Odyssey Dawn: A Model for Joint Experience, Training, and Education." *Joint Forces Quarterly* 64, 1st Qtr (2012): 24-29.

[2] Ibid., 26.

[3] Barak H. Obama, *National Security Strategy* (Washington, DC: White House, 2010).

[4] Carl von Clausewitz, *On War*, ed. and trans. Michael Howard and Peter Paret (Princeton: Princeton University Press, 1989), 75.

[5] Dan McCauley, "Wait a Minute – Just How Complex and Dangerous is it?", *Small Wars Journal*, Vol 8, No 12 (December 2012) http://smallwarsjournal.com/jrnl/art/wait-a-minute—just-how-complex-and-dangerous-is-it.

[6] U.S. Joint Forces Command, *The Joint Operating Environment 2010*, (Norfolk, VA: U.S. Joint Forces Command, February 2010), 66.

[7] Phil Williams, "Violent Non-State Actors and National and International Security", *International Relations and Security Network*, Zurich: Swiss Federal Institute of Technology (2008), 6.

[8] U.S. Department of Defense, *Irregular Warfare: Countering Irregular Threats Joint Operating Concept*, (Washington, DC: May 2010), 11, accessed via NWC 3032A.

[9] *JOE*, 61.

[10] Ibid.

[11] Justin Kelly and Mike Brennan, *Alien: How Operational Art Devoured Strategy*, Strategic Studies Institute (Carlisle, PA: U.S. Army War College, September 2009), 75.

[12] Chairman, U.S. Joint Chiefs of Staff, *Joint* Operations, Joint Publication (JP) 3-0, (Washington, DC: CJCS, 11 August 2011), II-3.

[13] James J. Schneider, *Vulcan Anvil: The American Civil War and the Foundations of Operational Art*, Theoretical Paper No. Four. (Fort Leavenworth, KS: U.S. School of Advanced Military Studies, June1992), 53.

[14] *JP 3-0*, II-4.

[15] Ibid., xii.

[16] Ibid., xiv.

[17] Chairman, U.S. Joint Chiefs of Staff, *Joint Operation Planning*, Joint Publication (JP) 5-0, (Washington, DC: CJCS, 11 August 2011), IV-1.

[18] Ibid., III-1.

[19] U.S. Department of the Army, *Army Leadership: Competent, Confident, and Agile*, Field Manual 6-22, (Washington, D.C: Government Printing Office 2006), 1-2.

[20] Ibid., 3-6.

[21] Ibid., 7-6.

[22] MilanVego, *Joint Operational Warfare: Theory and Practice* (Newport, RI: U.S. Naval War College, 2009), XI-39.

[23] Ibid., XI-35.

[24] Ibid., XI-36.

[25] Sooksan Kantabutra, "What Do We Know About Vision?" in *Leading Organizations: Perspectives for a New Era*, ed. Gill Robinson Hickman, (Thousand Oaks: SAGE Publications, Inc., 2010), 262.

[26] Chairman, U.S. Joint Chiefs of Staff, "Mission Command", *White Paper* (Washington, DC: CJCS, April 2012), 5.

18

[27] Robert M. Citino, *Blitzkrieg to Desert Storm: The Evolution of Operational Warfare.* (Kansas: University Printing Press of Kansas, 2004), 194.

[28] Ibid., 188.

[29] Ibid., 208.

[30] Ibid., 189.

[31] Ibid., 190.

[32] Ibid.

[33] Ibid., 211.

[34] Joshua Castellino, *International Law and Self-Determination: The Interplay of The Politics of Territorial Possession with Formulations of Post-Colonial National Identity.* (The Hague: Martinus Nijhoff Publishers, 2000), 148

[35] Ibid., 193.

[36] Ibid., 210.

[37] G.W. Choudhury. "Dismemberment of Pakistan, 1971: Its International Implications [Attempts to Examine the External Forces Connected with the Civil War in Bangladesh and the Third Indo-Pakistani War of 1971 and to Assess their Impact on the Emerging Balance of Power in South Asia]." Orbis 18, (1974): 190, accessed 2 April 2013, ProQuest.

[38] Citino, 210.

[39] Tommy Franks, *American Soldier.* (New York: Regan Books, 2004), 251-252.

[40] Senate Committee on Foreign Relations, *Tora Bora Revisited: How We Failed To Get Bin Laden And Why It Matters Today*, 111th Cong., 1st sess., 2009, Senate Print 111-35, 4, accessed 5 April 2013, http://www.gpo.gov/fdsys/pkg/CPRT-111SPRT53709/html/CPRT-111SPRT53709.HTM.

[41] Franks, 251.

[42] Rowan Scarborough, *Rumsfeld's War The Untold Story of America's Anti-Terrorist Commander* (Washington, DC: Regnery Publishing Inc., 2004), 31.

[43] Franks, 257.

[44] Seyom Brown and Robert H. Scales, ed., *US Policy in Afghanistan and Iraq: Lessons and Legacies* (Boulder, CO: Lynne Rienner Publishers, Inc., 2012), 1.

[45] Franks, 269.

[46] Ibid., 271.

[47] Thomas E. Ricks, *The Generals: American Military Command from World War II to Today* (New York: The Penguin Press, 2012), 399.

[48] *JP 5-0*, III-43-44

[49] General Tommy Franks, interview to Frontline, PBS, 2 June 2002 accessed on 10 April 2013, http://www.pbs.org/wgbh/pages/frontline/shows/campaign/interviews/franks.html.

[50] Ricks, 400.

[51] Chairman, U.S. Joint Chiefs of Staff, *Chairman's Strategic Direction to the Joint Force* (Washington, DC: CJCS, February 2012), 5-6.

[52] George W. Casey, Jr., *Strategic Reflections: Operation Iraqi Freedom, July 2004 - February 2007* (Washington, DC: National Defense University Press, October 2012), 156, accessed 2 April 2013 www.ndu.edu/press/strategicreflections.

[53] *JOE*, 70.

# BIBLIOGRAPHY

Brown, Seyom, and Robert Scales H. *US Policy in Afghanistan and Iraq: Lessons and Legacies*. Boulder, CO: Lynne Rienner Publishers, 2012.

Casey, George W. *Strategic Reflections: Operation Iraqi Freedom, July 2004-February 2007*. Washington, DC: National Defense University Press, 2012.

Castellino, Joshua. *International Law and Self-Determination: The Interplay of The Politics of Territorial Possession with Formulations of Post-Colonial National Identity*. The Hague: Martinus Nijhoff Publishers, 2000.

Connelly, Owen. On War and Leadership: *The Words of Combat Commanders from Frederick the Great to Norman Schwarzkopf*. Princeton, NJ: Princeton University Press, 2002.

Choudhury, G. W. *Dismemberment of Pakistan, 1971: Its International Implications*. Philadelphia: University of Pennsylvania, Foreign Policy Research Institute, 1974.

Citino, Robert Michael. *Blitzkrieg to Desert Storm: The Evolution of Operational Warfare*. Lawrence, Kan.: University Press of Kansas, 2004.

Clausewitz, Carl Von, Michael Howard Eliot, and Peter Paret. *On War*. Princeton, NJ: Princeton University Press, 1989.

Dempsey, Martin E. *Chairman's Strategic Direction to the Joint Force*. Washington, D.C.: Joint Chiefs of Staff, 2012.

_____. *Mission Command*. Washington, D.C.: Joint Chiefs of Staff, 2012.

Franks, Tommy. *American Soldier*. New York: Regan Books, 2004.

Hickman, Gill Robinson. *Leading Organizations: Perspectives for a New Era*. Los Angeles: SAGE Publications, 2010.

James, Gregory, Larry Holcomb, and Chad Manske. "Joint Task Force Odyssey Dawn: A Model for Joint Experience, Training, and Education." *Joint Forces Quarterly* 64, 1st Qtr (2012): 24-29.

Kerry, John. *"Tora Bora Revisited: How We Failed to Get Bin Laden and Why It Matters Today."* A Report to Members of the Committee on Foreign Relations, United States Senate, John Kerry, Chairman, One Hundred Eleventh Congress, First Session, November 30th, 2009. Washington, DC: Government Printing Office, 2009.

Kelly, Justin, and Mike Brennan. *Alien: How Operational Art Devoured Strategy*. Carlisle, PA: Strategic Studies Institute, U.S. Army War College, 2009.

Laver, Harry S. and Jeffrey J. Matthews. *The Art of Command: Military Leadership from George Washington to Colin Powell.* Lexington, KY: University Press of Kentucky, 2008

McCauley, Dan. "Wait a Minute – Just How Complex and Dangerous is it?", *Small Wars Journal*, Vol 8, No 12 (2012). http://smallwarsjournal.com/jrnl/art/wait-a-minute—just-how-complex-and-dangerous-is-it.

Obama, Barak H. *National Security Strategy*, Washington, DC: White House, May 2010. Accessed 4 March 2013. http://www.whitehouse.gov/sites/default/files/rss_viewer/national_security_strategy.pdf.

Pois, Robert A. and Phillip Langer. *Command Failure in War: Psychology and Leadership.* Bloomington, IN: Indiana University Press, 2004.

Ricks, Thomas E. *Fiasco: The American Military Adventure in Iraq.* New York, NY: Penguin Press, 2006.

_____. *The Generals: American Military Command from World War II to Today.* New York: Penguin Press, 2012.

Scarborough, Rowan. *Rumsfeld's War: The Untold Story of America's Anti-terrorist Commander.* Washington, D.C.: Regnery Pub., 2004.

Schneider, James J. *Vulcan's Anvil: The American Civil War and the Foundation of the Operational Art.* 1992.

Shuford, Jacob L. "Commanding at the Operational Level." Proceedings (United States Naval Institute) 133, no. 5 (May 2007): 22-29.

Taylor, Robert L. and William E. Rosenbach. *Military Leadership: In Pursuit of Excellence.* Cambridge, MA: Westview Press, 2005

U.S. Department of Army. *Army Leadership: Competent, Confident, and Agile.* Field Manual (FM) 6-22. Washington, DC: Headquarters, Department of Army, 2006.

U.S. Department of Defense. *Irregular Warfare: Countering Irregular Threats Joint Operating Concept.* Washington, DC: U.S. Department of Defense, 2010.

U.S. Joint Forces Command. *The Joint Operating Environment 2010.* Norfolk, VA: United States Joint Forces Command, 2010.

U.S. Office of the Chairman of the Joint Chiefs of Staff. *Joint Operations.* Joint Publication (JP) 3-0. Washington, DC: CJCS, 11 August 2011.

_____. *Joint Operation Planning.* Joint Publication (JP) 5-0. Washington, DC: CJCS, 11 August 2011.

Vego, Milan N. *Joint Operational Warfare: Theory and Practice*. Newport, RI: Naval War College, 2009.

Von Freytag-Loringhoven, Hugo Baron. *The Power of Personality in War*. Harrisburg, PA: Military Service Publishing Company, 1938.

Williams, Phil. "Violent Non-State Actors and National and International Security", *International Relations and Security Network*. Zurich: Swiss Federal Institute of Technology, 2008.

Wren, J. Thomas. *The Leader's Companion: Insights on Leadership through the Ages*. New York, NY: Free Press, 1995.

Zinni, Tony and Tony Koltz. *Leading the Charge*. New York, NY: Palgrave Macmillan, 2009.

General Tommy Franks, interview to Frontline, PBS, 2 June 2002 accessed on 10 April 2013, http://www.pbs.org/wgbh/pages/frontline/shows/campaign/interviews/franks.html.